I Share Creation

Bob Chilcott

for SATB choir and optional percussion

Vocal score

MUSIC DEPARTMENT

OXFORD
UNIVERSITY PRESS

OXFORD

UNIVERSITY PRESS

Great Clarendon Street, Oxford OX2 6DP, England
198 Madison Avenue, New York, NY10016, USA

Oxford University Press is a department of the University of Oxford.
It furthers the University's aim of excellence in research, scholarship,
and education by publishing worldwide in

Oxford New York
Auckland Bangkok Buenos Aires Cape Town Chennai
Dar es Salaam Delhi Hong Kong Istanbul Karachi Kolkata
Kuala Lumpur Madrid Melbourne Mexico City Mumbai Nairobi
São Paulo Shanghai Taipei Tokyo Toronto

Oxford is a registered trade mark of Oxford University Press
in the UK and in certain other countries

13

ISBN 0-19-335570-1   978-0-19-335570-5

Music and text origination by
Jeanne Roberts
Printed in Great Britain on acid-free paper by
Halstan & Co. Ltd., Amersham, Bucks.

Contents

Composer's note

In looking for texts that take a positive view and show respect for the environment, I was lucky to come across these short and strong poems. They all express to me a perspective that links man and nature in a way that shows humility, strength, and interdependence relative to our time.

The piece was commissioned jointly by The Reading Phoenix Choir and the National Environmental Research Council, and was first performed by the Reading Phoenix Choir at the Gala Concert of the Association of British Choral Directors in Guildford Cathedral, in August 2005.

Duration: *c.*8 minutes

Commissioned by Norman Morris and the Reading Phoenix Choir,
with support from the National Environmental Research Council,
and dedicated to Norman with affection.

I Share Creation

1. When the sun rises

Anon. Chinese (2500 BC)

BOB CHILCOTT

*Keyboard reduction for rehearsal only.

attacca

2. The Earth

Chief Seattle

attacca

3. *The Innermost House*

Anon. Aztec

I, the sing - er, lift them up, I, the sing - er, lift them up.

I, the sing - er, lift them up, I, the sing - er, lift them up,

I, the sing - er, lift them up, I, the sing - er, lift them up,

I, the sing - er, lift, lift them up, lift them up.

They are scat - tered,_____ they

They are scat - tered, scat - tered,_____ scat - - tered,

lift them up. They are scat - tered, scat - tered, scat - - tered,

lift them up. They are scat - tered, scat - - tered,

They, they are scat - tered, scat - - tered,

poco rit.
a tempo
58
f dim.
spread a - bout.
f
p
scat - tered, may wi - ther, may wi - ther, wi - ther, may wi - ther,
scat - - tered. Wi - ther, may wi - ther, wi - ther, may wi - ther,
scat - - tered.
poco rit.
a tempo
61
p
E - ven though on earth my flowers may wi - ther and
wi - ther, may wi - ther, wi - ther, may wi - ther, wi - ther, may wi - ther,
wi - ther, may wi - ther, wi - ther, may wi - ther, wi - ther, may wi - ther,
E - - - ven though my flowers may

for Ron Leishmann, 70 years young

4. Come to the great world

Anon. Arctic Inuit

fear feel - ing the cold, come to the great world, _____

fear feel - ing the cold, come to the great world, _____ and

_____ come to the great world, _____ and

come to the great world, _____

and see - ing _____ the moon, see - ing _____ the

see - ing _____ the moon, see - ing _____ the moon,

see - ing _____ the moon, see - - ing, se - ing _____ the

and see - - ing, se - ing _____ the moon,

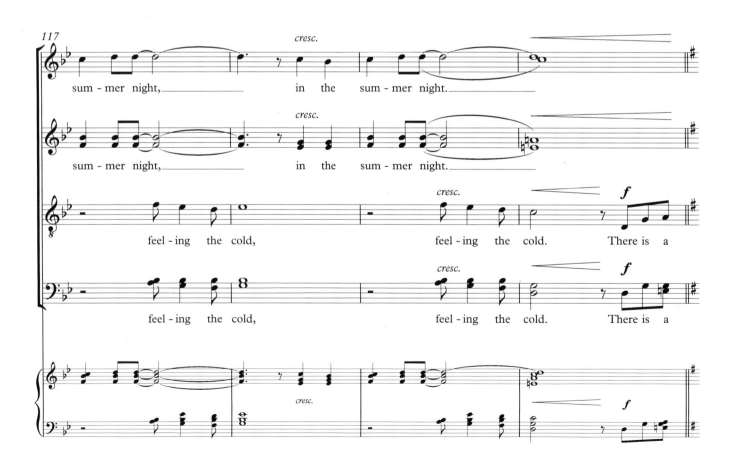

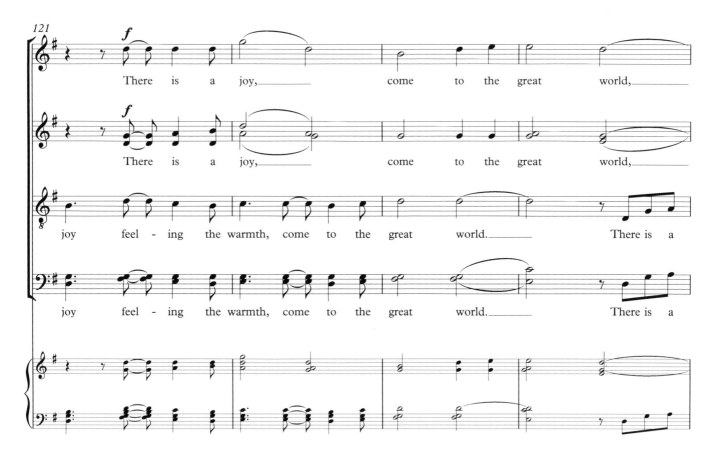

There is a joy,_____ come to the great world,_____

There is a joy,_____ come to the great world,_____

joy feel - ing the warmth, come to the great world._____ There is a

joy feel - ing the warmth, come to the great world._____ There is a

_____ feel - ing the joy, come to the great world, and

_____ feel - ing the joy, come to the great world, and

joy feel - ing the warmth, come_ to the great world,_____

joy feel - ing the warmth, come_ to the great world,_____

see - ing___ the sun, see - ing___ the sun,___

see - ing___ the sun, see - ing___ the sun,___

and see - ing___ the sun, see - ing___ the

and see - ing___ the sun, see - ing___ the

fol - low___ its foot - prints, fol - low___ its

fol - low___ its foot - prints, fol - low___ its

sun,___ fol - low___ its foot - prints,

sun,___ fol - low___ its foot - prints,

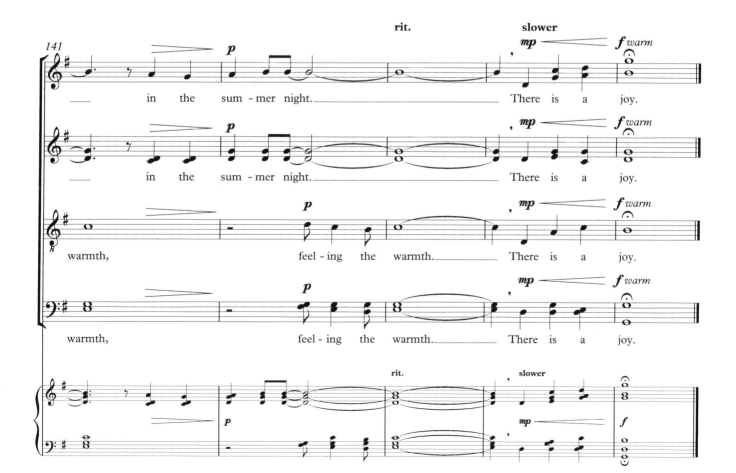